D0064968

COPING IN A CHANGING WORLD™

SUICIDE

Sandra Giddens

ROSEN
PUBLISHING®

New York

*With thanks to Frank, Harvey, Owen, Justine,
Kyle, and Merril*

Published in 2007 by The Rosen Publishing Group, Inc.
29 East 21st Street, New York, NY 10010

First Edition

Library of Congress Cataloging-in-Publication Data

Giddens, Sandra.
Suicide / by Sandra Giddens.—1st ed.
    p. cm.—(Coping in a changing world)
Includes bibliographical references.
ISBN-13: 978-1-4042-0952-7
ISBN-10: 1-4042-0952-2 (lib. bdg.)
1. Suicide. 2. Teenagers—Suicidal behavior. I. Title.
HV6545.G55 2007
362.28—dc22

2006024271

Printed in China

Contents

CHAPTER **ONE**

Suicide: Past to Present

SUICIDE IS A TRAGIC GLOBAL PUBLIC HEALTH PROBLEM. WORLDWIDE, MORE PEOPLE DIE FROM SUICIDE THAN FROM ALL HOMICIDES AND WARS COMBINED.

When someone says the word "suicide," it is usually met with silence. Just say the word, and immediately people want to avoid talking about the subject. Suicide describes the voluntary and intentional act of taking one's own life. It comes from two Latin root words, *sui* (of oneself) and *cidium* (a killing or slaying). It is very difficult to understand an act that is contrary to living one's day-to-day life. Most people want to experience aging, not to end their life prematurely.

Unfortunately, people are not transparent; you cannot look into their heads to see what they are thinking or feeling. Most people go through their day looking at people but not really seeing individuals. They might not notice that what they are seeing could be the person's cry for help. Is it the person who comes from the perfect family but feels that he or she does not measure up? Or is it someone who comes from an abusive family? Do you connect with the person who is always eating by him- or herself, an isolate? Do you see the person begging for help but not voicing it? Seeing people and connecting with them could be the first step in suicide prevention.

A teenager contemplating suicide may want to talk openly about his or her thoughts, but to them, society seems unwilling to hear them. The teen who is feeling isolated and in emotional pain may begin to feel more and more alone. Once someone in the family does commit suicide, the social stigma associated with the act makes recovery more difficult for the people who are left behind. If the teen could have had the opportunity to talk openly about his or her feelings, there might have been an opportunity to alter the outcome and save the teenager. By not keeping suicide under lock and key and trying to understand its occurrence, there could possibly be a means of preventing it from happening.

RELIGIOUS SUICIDES

Suicide is not a new phenomenon. In fact, it can be dated back to many cultures throughout history. Many of the earliest recordings of suicide can be found in the readings of the Bible. In the New Testament, for example, Judas, who betrayed Jesus, was so distraught that he hanged himself. In the Jewish Bible, Samson, once blinded by the Philistines, brings the temple down upon himself and the enemy.

MASS SUICIDES

In ancient times, suicide often occurred right after a battle so the enemy could not capture the conquered warriors. The thinking behind it was that they would rather take their own lives than be enslaved, mutilated, or tortured by their captors. In AD 73, hundreds of Jews died in what is generally believed to be a mass suicide on the top of Masada (in modern-day Israel), an ancient fortified plateau and the site of King Herod's palace, rather than being taken in and enslaved by the Romans.

They were said to have taken their own lives in one of three ways. First, the men embraced their wives and children and killed them. Next, lots were cast, and ten men were chosen to take the lives of the others. Finally, the last survivor set fire to the palace and took his own life.

Nine hundred and sixty men, women, and children died at Masada. When the Romans finally made it to the top of the plateau, they witnessed the bodies of those who chose death rather than be slaves to their enemies. The leader of the Jews, before the suicide, told his people, "Let us rather die, than be enslaved by our enemy. Let us leave this world in freedom."[1]

Mass suicides continued throughout history, many carried out not for the same reasons as the one at Masada. On November 18, 1978, a dynamic figure by the name of Jim Jones who headed the Peoples Temple religious cult ordered his followers to drink cyanide-laced juice. In all, 913 people killed themselves, including nearly 300 children. Jim Jones then shot himself in the head.

REGIONAL SUICIDES

There is a tribe in the South American rain forest called the Guarani-Kaiowa Indians whose suicide rate has been extremely high. In a ten-year period, about 200 Kaiowa are thought to have killed themselves. In 1995, as many as 56 of the 28,000 Kaiowa died in what are presumed to be suicides.[2]

It has been cited that the lack of land and poor life conditions contribute to the Guarani-Kaiowa Indians' taking of their own lives. It has also been a response to the Brazilian government, which was extinguishing their livelihoods by taking away their lands, forests, and, ultimately, beliefs. They live on small pieces of land totally unsuitable for agriculture and are forced to work in sugarcane plantations to survive. They earn very low salaries and spend a long time away from their loved ones.

In India, there was the suicide custom of suttee. Followers of Hinduism would burn their departed loved ones on funeral pyres. A wife was expected to throw herself over her husband's burning body as a final tribute of love and respect. Hindus had the belief system that the wife, once burned alive, would then proceed into the next life with her husband. It was abolished by law in British India in 1829, but isolated cases of voluntary suttee have occurred into the twenty-first century.

POLITICAL AND PATRIOTIC SUICIDES

Throughout history, there have been political suicides in which individuals would ignite themselves or starve themselves in protest. You have probably seen spies in Hollywood movies take suicide pills rather than be captured. This was in fact true. Many spies, of many nationalities throughout history, had orders not to divulge their secrets and to kill themselves before their secrets could be revealed to their enemies.

Seppuku was a ritual suicide and was considered an honorable death in Japanese culture. Warriors would perform seppuku to protect their honor. When they were on the brink of getting captured by their enemies, the troops would disembowel themselves, a practice called hara-kiri. This would ensure that the warriors' secrets died with them. When hara-kiri was done outside of a battle, it was a formal ceremony. The person would slice up his abdomen, stretch out his neck, and an assistant would then behead the person with one mighty sword stroke. The practice was banned in the seventeenth century.

During World War II (1939–1945), Japanese bomber pilots called kamikazes sacrificed their lives by going on suicidal missions that had them crashing their planes into set targets. They felt dying for their country was an honor, and they were considered national heroes. This idea that dying from an honorable death is better than living a life of disgrace continues into modern times.

THE CRIME, SIN, AND TRAGEDY OF SUICIDES

In eighteenth-century England, suicide was once considered a crime against the king because it deprived the ruler of collecting taxes. The victim was not allowed to be buried in sacred grounds, and the family's property was confiscated to pay the king for the losses. In the twentieth century, suicide was considered a crime in many U.S. states, though those who tried to commit suicide were rarely charged and brought to trial. One law in Massachusetts stated that a body of a person who had committed suicide was to be buried at a crossroads. Suicide is no longer considered illegal in that state.

Until recently, in Christian and Jewish traditions, suicide was looked upon as being shameful. Many family members would hide notes, weapons, and any evidence of suicide, and would even bribe coroners to alter the death certificates to hide the true cause of the death.

Playwrights write about suicide, but many times they romanticize it, like in *Romeo and Juliet*, by William Shakespeare. In some literature, videos, and movies, people are in love, tragedy strikes, one lover dies, and the other commits suicide as he or she does not want to live without his or her lover. In the twentieth century, despair and depression became a common element to many writers. Virginia Woolf, Dylan Thomas, Ernest Hemingway, and Jack London were just a few of the talented people who chose death by suicide.

Along with writers, there are many musicians who have killed themselves. The band Nirvana's frontman, Kurt Cobain, killed himself with a shotgun in 1994. People such as Jimi Hendrix, Janis Joplin, Sid Vicious, and Jim Morrison, to name a few, killed themselves by overdosing on drugs. Drug overdose may not necessarily be a deliberate act of suicide, but if these musicians had proper interventions, who knows what more they would have achieved in their lives? These artists' deaths must not be romanticized. They were talented people who had a lot to offer the world but ended their lives tragically and too soon.

CURRENT STATE OF SUICIDE

In 1897, sociologist Emile Durkheim theorized in his book *Suicide: A Study in Sociology* that suicide rates increase when a society's value system breaks down. The Great Depression (1929–1939) saw an increase in suicides. Many men sank into despair after they could not find jobs. The suicide rate increased from 14 to 17 per 100,000.[3]

Taking one's life has occurred throughout history. Even today, news stories tell of people taking their own lives. Young suicide bombers give up their lives for what they see as noble causes. Suicide continues to be a major concern in today's society, and the problem is not lessening or going away.

If you ask most people, they know one or more friends, family members, famous stars, or acquaintances who have ended their lives through the act of suicide. Suicide is the eighth leading cause of death in the United States. It is estimated that five million people now living in the United States have attempted suicide. The World Health Organization (WHO) estimates that the suicide rate worldwide could rise to 1.5 million suicides per year by the year 2020. Dr. Catherine Le Galès-Camus of WHO says, "Suicide is a tragic global public health problem. Worldwide, more people die from suicide than from all homicides and wars combined."[4]

Teen Suicide Statistics

It is very frightening when you look at suicide statistics for young men and women. Look at the face of a clock and start counting. Approximately once every eighty seconds a teenager attempts suicide, and approximately once every 100 minutes a teen actually succeeds. In 1997, in a Youth and Risk Behavior Survey, half of all high school students reported that they had seriously considered suicide by the time they had graduated. This means that millions of students reported they had contemplated doing it. After car accidents and murder, suicide is the third leading cause of death for fifteen- to twenty-four-year-olds in the United States.[5]

Suicide rates among ten- to fourteen-year-olds have nearly doubled in the past few decades. White teenage boys have the highest rate of suicide. Black teenagers are now more than twice as likely to kill themselves as they were twenty years ago. Out of every five people who commit suicide, four are likely to be male. Females are three times more likely to attempt suicide, but males are the ones who succeed at their attempts. Males tend to use more violent methods, like shooting themselves, than women do. A woman might use pills, so, therefore, some can be saved. Recently, many teenage girls who have died by suicide have used violent methods like guns. Gun deaths continue to be on a steady climb. Frighteningly, nearly 60 percent of all suicides in the United States are committed with a gun.

The rate of suicide for teens may even be higher than reported. Automobile crashes account for the leading cause of death for fifteen- to nineteen-year-olds. Law enforcement officials might look at a car crash of a single teenage driver, see no skid marks, and put down the cause as "accident." In fact, these car crashes could be "autocides," the term for suicide by car crash.

For a number of teens, the transition into adulthood can be difficult. Adolescents can be a particularly vulnerable group that can encounter pressure from their family and peer group. Many often encounter some of the following pressures and problems:

- Family breakdown
- Sexuality (teenage pregnancy, sexually transmitted diseases, sexual identity issues)
- Body image (anorexia nervosa, bulimia, obesity, acne)
- Moral and spiritual (conflict with parental values, rebellion, susceptibility to religious groups and cults)
- School achievement
- Peer pressure
- Social challenges

These problems may result in further stress to the adolescent that could lead to a state of depression, which is the most common cause of suicide.

CHAPTER TWO

Depression

THOSE AGED FIFTEEN TO
TWENTY-FOUR SUFFER THE
HIGHEST RATE OF DEPRESSION
AND SUICIDAL THOUGHTS, AND
YET, THEY ARE ALSO THE LEAST
LIKELY TO SEEK OUTSIDE HELP
OF ANY AGE GROUP.

Depression continues to be the most frequently noted effect in presuicidal and suicidal young men and women.[1] The majority of people who kill themselves are depressed. Of people who commit suicide, 90 percent have at least one psychiatric disorder. Clinical depression is the most common disorder.[2]

Those aged fifteen to twenty-four suffer the highest rate of depression and suicidal thoughts, and yet, they are also the least likely to seek outside help of any age group. There is a direct link between depressive illnesses and suicide. It is important to note that teens who are feeling depressed do not necessarily take it to the next step of wanting to stop living. It is also very important to note that teens feeling depressed need help and support.

It is not unusual to feel sad, blue, or even depressed from time to time. Sadness is a normal reaction to loss or grieving. Sometimes these emotions of feeling down in the dumps are so intense that they interfere with one's day-to-day living. People can get depressed for many reasons: loss of a personal relationship, illness, grief, feeling alone, poor self-esteem, feeling like a failure in life, abusing alcohol and drugs, or a number of intense life disappointments.

SIGNS OF DEPRESSION

Depression is an internal state. The image people who are depressed project to the rest of the world may not reveal the true desperation they are, in fact, experiencing internally. Some exhibit a few, and some experience many, of the following signs of depression:

- Losing interest in hobbies, school, and friends
- Complaining about a lot of aches and pains
- Feeling blue, rebellious, and angered
- Sleeping too much or too little
- Letting hygiene go
- Low energy
- Crying spells
- Trouble with day-to-day concentration or memory
- Persistent sad, anxious, or empty mood
- Feelings of hopelessness and pessimism
- Feelings of guilt, worthlessness, and helplessness
- Decreased energy and fatigue
- Difficulty making decisions
- Weight loss or gain
- Restlessness and irritability
- Persistent symptoms such as headaches, digestive disorders, and chronic pain
- Thoughts of death and suicide
- Suicide attempts

SYMPTOMS OF ADOLESCENT DEPRESSION

- Crying
- Low self-esteem
- Loss of energy, fatigue
- Sleep disturbance

- Sadness
- Guilt/remorse
- Restlessness
- Health-related complaints
- Irritability
- Helplessness/hopelessness
- Lowered concentration
- Appetite change
- Sulkiness
- Self-reproach
- Loss of interest
- Weight loss or gain
- Withdrawal
- Aggressiveness

Any of these characteristics may be common in teenagers, but the time to be concerned is when roughly five or more are prevalent.

Studies of causes and treatment for depression are constantly being done. Here are a few causes that have been identified:

- Chemical imbalances in the brain
- Chronic illnesses
- Side effects of medication
- Hormonal changes in the body
- Alcohol and drug abuse
- Trauma

TYPES OF DEPRESSION

There are different kinds of depression. A less severe kind of depression is when you may be feeling emotionally down or sad but not for an extended period of time. You may start eating more or less and do not feel really energetic. This is a temporary state, and you usually bounce back again.

In seasonal affective disorder (SAD), people who have difficulties adjusting to less sunlight during the winter months feel depressed and blue. Bipolar disorder is a mental disorder that can be seen as a wide variance of mood. This disturbance sometimes consists of depression or of mania, which is when a person is hyperactive, highly elated, or irritable. Someone who is bipolar has mood swings between these two states.

Clinical depression means that the depression is severe enough to require treatment. A person who is clinically depressed feels sad most of the day, nearly every day, for at least two weeks. Often the person cannot sleep or sleeps too much. Clinically depressed people lose interest in activities that they once enjoyed, lose their sense of value for themselves, and feel worthless and helpless. Because they have a severe loss or increase in appetite, a weight change may start to become noticeable. For adolescents, depression may appear like irritability. Self-destructive behavior may be common when dealing with depressive states. This behavior may take more indirect forms as in acting out and self-destructive behaviors such as cutting (using a knife on the skin) or alcohol and drug abuse. Attempting suicide is a more direct and highly lethal form. Clinically depressed adolescents are five times more likely to attempt suicide than their nondepressed peers.[3] In treating clinical depression, many professionals work with antidepressant medications. Depression and signs of depression should be taken very seriously. The sooner it can be identified and treated, the better it is for everyone concerned.

BULLYCIDE AND DEPRESSION

Jared's mother, Belinda High, has a Web site entitled JaredStory.com. She became an advocate for suicide prevention after the suicide of her beloved son, Jared. Here's what she wrote about her son's suicide.

> *It is believed that depression causes most suicides, but this creates a new question—what causes the depression? A person just doesn't wake up one morning with depression. Psychologists believe that some people have a genetic tendency toward depression, some develop depression because of environmental triggers, and some people can have both genetic and environmental triggers. Jared developed depression from bullying at school as well as an assault by a bully in school. The new term being used to describe this type of teen suicide is "bullycide," a suicide caused by the effects of bullying. Jared's loss by bullycide on September 29, 1998, filled our lives with grief, but the healing has come. We were left behind with only memories of Jared, some good, some bad, but our healing journey goes on.[4]*

CHAPTER THREE

Risk Factors

TEENS SEE GAMBLING AS A WAY TO MAKE A QUICK BUCK; WHAT THEY CANNOT ENVISION IS THE CYCLE OF LOSING AND GOING INTO DEBT . . . THEY START CRAVING THE THRILL OF THE WIN AND OF COURSE GET DESPONDENT, OR LET DOWN, AT THE LOSS.

Many teens go through their lives dealing with their responsibilities in appropriate ways. There are those, however, who will get themselves in risky situations and have difficulties coping with them. Risk factors are circumstances that may predispose a person to consider or attempt suicide. It is important to note that not all risk factors lead to suicide.

Some of the main risk factors include:

- Alcohol and drug abuse
- Gambling
- School and/or personal crisis
- Setting high standards for oneself
- Legal problems
- Social isolation
- Trouble at home
- Bullying
- Unplanned pregnancy
- Previous suicide attempt
- Depression
- Media influence and cluster suicides (copycat suicides)
- New situations like beginning college
- Chemical imbalances
- Early traumas
- Sexual identity issues

ALCOHOL AND DRUG ABUSE

Drugs and alcohol are additional complicating factors in an adolescent's world. They are used by many teens to attempt to reduce the pain they are feeling from stress and feelings of helplessness or hopelessness. Teens can start feeling signs of depression as early as age twelve or thirteen. If they do not seek professional help, depressed teens may seek out other methods to relieve themselves of their symptoms. They may turn to drugs and alcohol to help them deal with their pain. Teens who engage in high-risk behaviors involving sex and alcohol and drugs have significantly higher odds of suicidal thoughts and suicide attempts.

When a person first starts to drink alcohol, it can elevate the mood, but it is in fact a depressant drug. Having two to three glasses of alcohol can impair one's vision, speech, coordination, and sense of balance, and can cause loss of self-control. If a teen already suffers from depression, alcohol can increase his or her feelings. If a teen is feeling suicidal, these feelings may become enhanced after drinking alcohol. The relationship between alcoholism and suicide appears to be stronger among males than females. Studies show that among young people who took their own lives, the drugs most commonly abused after alcohol were marijuana, cocaine, amphetamines, and combinations of these. As well, young people who have not been known to have suicidal feelings before may become vulnerable to depression and suicidal emotions under the influence of chemicals, particularly after prolonged use.

The National Longitudinal Study of Adolescent Health analyzed survey data in the mid-1990s from 132 U.S. schools, looking at the sex and drug behavior patterns of 19,000 seventh to twelfth graders. The researchers clustered the adolescents into groups according to their behavior. Abstainers had the lowest levels of depression, suicidal thoughts, and suicide attempts. Teens in groups associated with sex and heavy use of illegal drugs like marijuana had the highest level. It was also found that girls compared to boys were less likely to pursue high-risk behaviors, but when they did, they were more vulnerable to depression, suicidal thoughts, and suicide attempts.

The results indicate that high-risk behaviors can contribute to suicidal behavior in many teenagers. Young people who are depressed could also be more drawn to drugs as a form of self-medication and escape. Autopsies of adolescent suicide victims show that one-third to one-half of teenagers were under the influence of drugs or alcohol before they killed themselves.[1]

GAMBLING

A high school student in New York bet on a World Series game with the campus bookie. He lost and owed the bookie $6,000. His wealthy parents could have paid for it, but he was too ashamed to tell them. He took out a gun and

*pointed it at his head. In his pocket he left a
suicide note.*[2]

Gamblers have the highest suicide rate of any
addicted group. Although teens cannot gamble
legally, they find ways by going to casinos and
gambling Web sites, using campus bookies to put
money down on sports games, and betting on
cards at school. Presently, poker is the new rage
with teenagers. Many stay up all night online or
attend gambling parties. Teens see gambling as a
way to make a quick buck; what they cannot envision is the cycle of losing and going into debt. Many
teens who constantly play on the Internet, sometimes winning and many times losing, are isolated.
They start craving the thrill of the win and of
course get despondent, or let down, at the loss.

SCHOOL AND PERSONAL PROBLEMS

School can certainly be stressful for some teens.
There is the stress of passing tests, completing
day-to-day homework, getting into a college or
university, being popular, and basically fitting in.
There are also the physical, sexual, and emotional
changes that occur through adolescence. This is
the time for change and discovery. It is also a time
for moods to be somewhat erratic. Most of this is
quite normal. It is when a teen is feeling out of
control and in crisis that the need for help sooner
than later must occur.

Some school problems can be attributed to the student having difficulties with the academics, perhaps because the student has a learning disability. At times, school problems can be a warning sign of deeper issues. It may be a sign that the teen is feeling depressed.

Adolescence is also the time when young men and women start getting romantically involved. With relationships also come breakups. There are incidents in which teens of both genders have attempted suicide because they could not cope with their romantic breakups. This has been more prevalent among females.

Young women are also more prone to anorexia nervosa, an eating disorder in which people restrict their food intake. In some cases, anorexia leads to death, a slow suicide.

Many teens feel there is an in crowd and that they are not part of it. If the teen cannot make any friends, this can be cause for concern. Many people can look around and identify peers who are loners. Many times teens do not empathize or put themselves in the other person's shoes. The loners may not want to be that way but have not found a way to break in to a crowd, or perhaps they use their aloneness to hide their own insecurities.

Some students who take their own lives are indeed the opposite of the rebellious teen. Setting high standards and not achieving them as well as family pressures of setting overly high expectations to excel can also be problems. These are anxious, insecure students who have a desperate desire to be liked, to fit in, and to do well. Their expectations are so high that they demand too much of themselves and are condemned to constant disappointment. Being a teenager is not an easy experience. There are times when you are feeling up and times when you are feeling down. It is when the down times and the negative feelings start to take over that the need to get help and support is crucial.

PARENT-CHILD BREAKDOWN

The relationship between parent and child is a significant family relationship. Many researchers trace suicidal feelings and behavior to long-term depressive illness rooted in very dysfunctional parent-child relationships.[3]

In a study by the American Academy of Pediatrics, adult women who said they were physically or emotionally abused as children were more likely to have mental problems, to suffer from depression, and to have attempted suicide.[4]

For suicidal children, a significant number of their parents are unable to express emotions, frequently punish their children when they don't meet their high expectations, are abusive, are seldom around their children, are mentally ill, or are addicted to drugs and alcohol.[5]

The breakup of the two-parent family, whether from divorce, desertion, or the death of a parent, makes children more vulnerable. Children's advocates still maintain it's the quality of the parenting not the makeup of the family that matters most.

Suicidal behavior does not necessarily happen all at once. A family's background and circumstances may predispose the teen to suicidal behavior. The factor of marriage and separation is highly correlated with suicidal behavior. Within families, social, economic, personal, and behavioral factors can cause stress or depression that may predispose members to suicide. Suicidal behavior may run in families.

DIFFICULTY AT BIRTH

Children's doctor Lee Salk and his team were interested in seeing if birth complications and suicide were connected. He looked at the birth records of 52 people born between 1957 and 1967, all of whom had committed suicide, with a control group of 104 people also born between 1957 and 1967 who were not suicidal. After looking at the data, he discovered three characteristics of the group that had committed suicide.

1. Born to a mother who received very little to no prenatal care
2. Born to a mother who suffered chronic disease in pregnancy

3. Experienced respiratory distress at least one hour before being born

Salk and his team estimated that at least 60 percent of teens who committed suicide had at least one of these characteristics. His theory on the third characteristic was that there might have been neurological damage that made the person unable to deal with the stresses of life. For numbers 1 and 2, it is possible that the mother may have not wanted prenatal care because she may have been ambivalent about wanting the baby. Other possibilities are that the ill mother could only focus on herself and not her newborn, or could not afford treatment.[6]

In 1998, Bertil Jacobson and Marc Bygdeman found flaws in Salk's study and did their own research. They looked at perinatal conditions (traumatic birth) that caused pain to the fetus. The two researchers found that certain conditions were associated with an increased risk of suicide by violent means for adult men later in their life. They concluded that minimizing pain and discomfort during birth seems to be important in reducing the risk of committing suicide by violent means as an adult.

Jacobson also discovered that risk factors may not only provide the urge to commit suicide but how one attempts it. He found that those individuals who killed themselves through the manner of hanging, drowning, strangulation, or carbon monoxide poisoning were four times more likely to have had loss of oxygen at birth than his control group.[7]

It does appear that there may be a relationship between trauma at birth and people at risk for suicide later on in their lives. More studies and research are still necessary on this topic.

CHAPTER FOUR
Bullying, Cyberbullying, and Rock and Roll

MANY STUDENTS WHO KILL THEMSELVES WERE BULLIED BY OTHERS AND COULD NOT BREAK THE HEARTBREAKING CYCLE. SUICIDE WAS A WAY OUT FROM THE DAY-TO-DAY TORMENT.

Bullying incidents have been reported during all levels in school from primary grades to high schools. Bullying incidents have also been reported at the college level and even in the workforce. Many school boards have curriculum that addresses the problem of bullying. Some have help lines to assist the victims.

If you have ever been bullied, you cannot help but feel disempowered. On the other hand, if you have actually bullied another person, you may feel strong, powerful, and controlling. If you have been at the side, watching, not interfering, as the bullying occurs, you may feel a range of these emotions. Many students who kill themselves were bullied by others and could not break the heartbreaking cycle. Suicide was a way out from the day-to-day torment.

CYBERBULLYING

The Internet has created a whole new world of communication for people. Young people gravitate to their computers to talk to friends on instant messaging servers like MSN, make their own personal blogs, or do text messaging on their computers or cell phones. Media Awareness Network research shows that 50 percent of students say they are alone online most of the time. Only about 16 percent say they talk to their parents a lot about what they do online. Because bullies tend to harass their victims away from the watchful eye of an adult, the Internet has provided the perfect tool to reach others, bully them, and many times remain anonymous. The frightening part of this is that the home can no longer be a refuge for the victim.

While most interactions online are positive, there are those who use this form of communication in a very negative manner. They antagonize and intimidate people. This has become known as cyberbullying. It is a way to harass, humiliate, or threaten others using the Internet or cell phones. There are cases in which cyberbullying has been one of the main causes for young people to end their lives by committing suicide.

> *A group of girls had been taunting Alan through instant messaging (IM), teasing him about how small he was and daring him to do things. They dared him to commit suicide. On IM he discussed suicide with them. They led him to think it was a great joke. One afternoon, Alan jumped off a high bridge. He had deleted everything from his computer, except the one message, "The only way to get the respect you deserve is to die."[1]*

One method of bullying involves taking pictures on cell phones. It operates like this: Someone takes a picture of a peer, then the bully puts the picture on the Internet and either attaches it to different bodies or manipulates the photo of the peer into compromising poses, sometimes pornographic ones. The victim then discovers that he or she is plastered all over the Internet and is humiliated and wants to hide from life.

Another form of bullying is when the person is locked out from everyone's messaging servers.

No one will accept him or her. That person feels isolated and degraded. The laugh people have on the victim can be tragic in the end for all.

Cyberbullying can be hard to control because most adults are not aware of what is going on in chat rooms or messaging centers. It is important that your parents look at what messaging name and picture you are using. Some teens may be putting themselves in poses that look like soft porn thinking that it is funny. They also may be using nicknames that are sensational and sensual. Representing yourself in these manners could get the attention of people who don't regard this behavior as funny but as an invitation to contact you. It is important that your parents are aware of what you are doing and receiving on the Internet.

MUSIC

One area that has received considerable attention deals with the effect of song lyrics and music videos on teens' behavior. Heavy metal and rap lyrics can be very provocative. These forms of music often express concern over social problems but rarely do they offer solutions or hope for the situations. In 1973, Alice Cooper performed a mock suicide, and some felt that this led to some adolescents attempting suicide or just wanting to copy the act.

There have been cases brought to court in which parents have made accusations that the songs their teens listened to drove their children to commit suicide. In a 1985 case, teens James Vance and his friend Raymond Belknap were drinking and listening to *Stained Class*, an album by the British heavy metal group Judas Priest. They went to their local cemetery and took turns shooting themselves. Belknap killed himself right then. Vance survived, but three years later, he killed himself. The families of both boys sued Judas Priest and CBS Records, but the court ruled in favor of the band's rights to free speech.

In 1986, there was another suit in which the father of a teenage boy sued Ozzy Osbourne, claiming that his son committed suicide after listening to the song "Suicide Solution." The court again ruled in favor of Osbourne's rights to free speech.

MEDIA

The media can impact and influence society, but the question is, can the media's extensive coverage of suicides promote copycat suicides? Several studies have tried to answer this question. According to the Irish Association of Suicidology, evidence suggests that inappropriate reporting or depiction can in fact lead to an escalation of suicidal behaviors.[2]

A 1986 study looked at an episode of the British soap opera *EastEnders* in which a character attempts suicide by overdose. In the week the program was aired, there was a marked increase in the number of people admitted to the hospital for overdosing.[3]

Ira Wasserman started studying imitation and suicide, particularly looking at celebrity suicides. He discovered that there was a significant correlation between celebrity suicides and subsequent suicides in society.[4]

In 1999, two students shot twelve students, a teacher, and themselves at Columbine High School in Colorado. Within six weeks after the school shooting, six students killed themselves in Los Angeles County in California. In four of the cases in which suicide notes were left, three mentioned Columbine as inspiration. "If you plaster their face up on the news for 20 minutes, that's going to make the difference," said Dr. William Pollack of Harvard. Media coverage of suicides isn't the reason for a child's decision to kill him- or herself, Dr. Pollack says, but it's a contributing factor.[5]

CLUSTER SUICIDES

Cluster suicides are suicides that take place in a specific geographic area over a short period of time, sometimes as the result of a suicide pact. Many instances involve lovers, friends, or family members. Cluster suicides occur predominantly with adolescents and young adults, and they account for up to 5 percent of all suicides that succeed in this age group.[6]

In Japan, six young people were found dead in a car from asphyxiation in 2006. The five men and one woman, whose deaths were suspected as suicides, met online and arranged a pact to kill themselves. This example in Japan is one of many such pacts that have taken place everywhere around the globe, from Guam to the Netherlands, since the 1990s. Many of the victims of suicide pacts met in chat rooms in which the participants exchanged ideas about how to kill themselves.

CHAPTER FIVE

Groups at Risk

ROBBIE KIRKLAND HAD GROWN WEARY OF BEING DIFFERENT. HE WAS GAY, AND IN ROBBIE KIRKLAND'S MIND, DEATH SEEMED LIKE THE EASIER OPTION.

T here are a number of high-risk groups that are vulnerable and show more incidents of depression and suicidal thoughts than other groups. Some of these groups are Native American teens, Native Canadian teens, African American teens, Hispanic and Latino teens, gay or bisexual teens, and teens with Asperger's syndrome.

In 1998, white Americans accounted for 84 percent of all youth suicides. Out of the 84 percent, 61 percent were males and 23 percent were females. The suicide rate for Native Americans was 19.3 per 100,000 in that year, higher than the 8.5 per 100,000 overall average. For African Americans, the suicide rate has increased more than two-fold since 1980. Latino high-schoolers are twice as likely to attempt suicide than their white counterparts.[1] It has been estimated that gay teens are four times more at risk of suicide than their heterosexual counterparts.

NATIVE CANADIANS AND NATIVE AMERICANS

It isn't unusual to see Native Canadian children as young as six years old playing a game called Suicide in Ontario, Canada. Suicide is played by having one player tie a rope around his or her opponent's neck until the victim yells, "Suicide!"[2]

From 1979 through 1992, 4,718 Native Americans who resided on or near reservations died from violence—2,324 from homicides and 2,394 from suicide. During this fourteen-year period, overall homicide rates for Native Americans were about two times higher than usual and 1.5 times higher than U.S. national rates.[3]

Today, the suicide rate is still substantially higher among Native teens. Depression and suicide are huge problems among Native teens. They have to live in a world where racism is on the rise, and they struggle to fit in.

When teens feel there is nowhere to go, some turn to inhaling gasoline, alcohol abuse, and drugs to deal with their depression. Drug and alcohol abuse affect up to 70 percent of the First Nations Canadian tribal population. Suicide occurs roughly five to six times more often among First Nations youth than other youth in Canada.[4] The ratio of young men to young women who commit suicide is four to one.

In the Mushuau Innu Native Canadian village of Labrador, Canada, there are six graves in this 700-person town that was founded in 2002. Out of the six townspeople who have died, drunken driving claimed the lives of five young people, three of whom had committed suicide.[5]

Native Americans and Native Canadians have specific risk factors, such as:

- Economic marginalization (being poor)
- Rapid culture change and/or cultural discontinuity (their life as they once knew it is rapidly disappearing)

- Forced assimilation (being absorbed by society)
- Forced relocation (being forced off their native lands)
- School experience that gave exposure to violence and abuse at a young age
- Copycat suicidal behaviors due to the close ties and identification among youth in these small communities.[6]

In an attempt to turn the situation around, efforts are continually being made to help these youth help themselves through education, support groups, and treatment facilities and programs.

BLACK AND LATINO TEENS

Though the risk of suicide among young people is still highest with white males, suicide rates more than doubled among black youths between 1980 and 1995.[7] For fifteen- to nineteen-year-old black males, the rate has increased more than 100 percent. For all other groups during the same period, the increase was 11 percent. Firearm deaths, which are responsible for a majority of teen homicides and suicides but also include accidental deaths, were highest in 2003 among blacks (59.4 males per 100,000 and 4.2 females per 100,000).[8]

Black and Latino teens from lower socioeconomic backgrounds reported that they had suicidal thoughts and said they had few adults in their lives with whom they could discuss their personal problems. Those who attempted suicide were more than twice as likely to report that they had no one to count on compared to a non-suicidal group.

HOMOSEXUALITY

During the early morning hours of Thursday, January 2, fourteen-year-old Robbie Kirkland walked through his sister Claudia's bedroom and climbed the stairs to the attic. He had gone into his father's room earlier the same day, where he found the key to the lock on his father's gun. Before walking away with the weapon and some ammunition, he put the keys back exactly where he had found them.

Alone with his secret and the loaded gun, Robbie decided once and for all to put an end to the life that caused him so much sadness and confusion. Pulling the trigger, he reasoned, would stop the turmoil he felt inside. He wouldn't have to keep his secret any more. Robbie Kirkland had grown weary of being different. He was gay, and in Robbie Kirkland's mind, death seemed like the easier option.[9]

A U.S. government's study, titled *Report of the Secretary's Task Force on Youth Suicide*, found that gay youth are two to three times more likely to attempt suicide than other young people. In a study of 8,000 Seattle, Washington, high school students, gay and lesbian teens were three times more at risk for suicide attempts than heterosexual students.[10]

Several researchers have suggested that youths who are bisexual or uncertain of their sexual orientation may be at an even higher risk for suicidal behavior than self-proclaimed homosexual teenagers.

YOUNG PEOPLE WITH ASPERGER'S SYNDROME

Asperger's syndrome is a neurological disorder that is generally classified as a form of autism. People with Asperger's have the intellectual capacity of those without the syndrome, but they exhibit deficiencies in social and communication skills. Though not a lot is clear about Asperger's (this syndrome has been known since 1944), it appears to be more common in males. Though there is no treatment or cure for Asperger's yet, many people with this disease often go through rehabilitation therapy of some kind.

Due to difficulties in making friends and feeling socially excluded, depression and other secondary psychiatric disorders can be especially common among people with forms of autism and Asperger's syndrome. There is a higher than average incidence of suicide within this population.

CHAPTER SIX

Myths, Warning Signs, and Guidelines

ONE OF THE MOST SERIOUS SIGNS OF IMPENDING SUICIDE IS WHEN A PERSON HAS BEEN DEPRESSED FOR A LONG TIME OR HAS ALREADY HAD A SUICIDE ATTEMPT AND SUDDENLY HE OR SHE CHEERS UP. THIS COULD BE A SIGN THAT HE OR SHE HAS MADE A DECISION TO TRY TO DIE.

ontrary to popular beliefs that suicides occur around holidays, such as Thanksgiving, Christmas, and New Year's, research indicates that spring is the most popular time for suicide. Suicide is usually committed during the daytime. Less than 30 percent of people who commit suicide leave a note. Many times, suicide attempts are actually cries for help. The act is a way of communicating the intense turmoil the person is feeling. Many teens do not actually want to end their lives; they want an end to the pain they are feeling.

A key to coping with suicidal thoughts and helping people who are suicidal is to understand the desire to take one's life. To further understand, it would be beneficial to look at the myths connected with the topic.

COMMON MYTHS AND FACTS

Myth: All suicidal people fully intend to die.

Fact: It is not necessarily true that all suicidal people truly want to end their lives. Many do so and choose methods that are very lethal, such as guns to the head, but there are those who choose methods, such as pills, that may signal a cry for help. They may want to live but not under the prevailing circumstances in which they have found themselves.

Myth: Friends should not tell on a friend who is talking about suicide.

Fact: It is difficult to betray a friend's trust, and you may feel he or she is going to be angry with you, but by telling a responsible adult, you may in fact be saving your friend's life. This is one secret you should not keep!

Myth: Once a teen is suicidal, he or she is considered suicidal for his or her entire life.

Fact: Many times people can feel suicidal for a limited time, and with the proper interventions and preventive measures, their behavior can be controlled. It is important to note that being suicidal is not necessarily a life sentence.

Myth: People who talk about suicide will not attempt it.

Fact: People who talk about suicide do quite often attempt and even succeed at killing themselves. If a teenager mentions that he or she is thinking of suicide, do not brush or laugh it off; take the threat very seriously. Eighty percent of people give many clues to the fact that they are going to attempt to take their own lives. This means that if you know ten people who constantly talk about suicide, eight of those ten may try it, so take it seriously.

Myth: Suicide is hereditary.

Fact: Some families do have a history of suicide. Suicidal behavior is not necessarily predetermined genetically, but there is a major concern that once a suicide exists in a family, other members may be at high risk. What is hereditary is a predisposition for depression, which can lead to suicidal thoughts. There also may be a chemical imbalance in the body or brain that is caused by a genetic abnormality. Nowadays, with medication and counseling, high-risk family members can be helped. Mental disorders are a factor in more than half of the suicides in North America. People bereaved by suicide, especially family members, are eight times more likely to commit suicide themselves.

Myth: People who survive a suicide attempt never try again.

Fact: Half of all teens who have made one suicide attempt will make another, sometimes as many as two a year until they succeed. In fact, three months after the first attempt, repeat attempts have been noted to occur, even when it looks like the person may be improving. That is the strange thing—just when you think the person looks happier, he or she may try and take his or her own life again. The issues and the problems that led to the suicide attempt need to be altered or changed, otherwise the person may likely try again. The majority of suicide attempts are expressions of extreme distress and not just harmless bids for attention. Those teens who have had a suicide attempt should be carefully monitored.

Myth: Every death is preventable.

Fact: No matter how well intentioned, how alert, and how caring people are, there is no way of preventing all suicides from happening.

Myth: People from good families never commit suicide.

Fact: Suicide can claim people from all walks of life, religion, socioeconomic stature, and age. For example, a teenager may feel that he or she is in a perfect family but feels he or she can never be good enough.

Myth: Suicide is painless.

Fact: Many suicide methods are in fact painful. The media sometimes portray suicide attempts romantically, but the reality is they can be very harsh.

WHAT ARE THE WARNING SIGNS?

Young people who have attempted suicide exhibit classic warning signs. When people talk about suicide, listen, as it can be a cry for help. When a teen starts making comments like he or she soon will not be hurting anymore, people will be sorry when he or she is gone, and everyone would be better off without him or her, these should make you concerned. Some other worrying signs are when your friend starts asking questions about dying, such as whether you think dying hurts. Your friend may indicate that he or she wants the sadness and depression to go away and may want to do something about it. These are cries for help, and they must be heard.

Some other signs that need immediate response include constantly talking about his or her own death, asking about different ways to kill oneself (learning the amount of a lethal dose of medication, how to get a gun, etc.), and actually saying he or she wants to commit suicide. Your friend may be preoccupied with books and music that have the common theme of suicide or be busy planning his or her own funeral. Obvious signs are when the person starts putting affairs in order, making his or her final wishes known to friends and family, and giving away personal belongings.

Sometimes people may be influenced by someone close to them who has recently committed suicide. The grief over the loved one may be so overwhelming that they see suicide as the only answer.

If you see the signs of depression after an event like this, the person should be persuaded to seek help.

It is always a concern when people appear to be withdrawn, with little interest about things and events around them. There is a reason to worry when the physical well-being of people starts to impact their day-to-day living, such as disruptive sleeping patterns (either too much or too little sleep), abnormal eating habits, and poor grooming, such as neglect of appearance. Persistent boredom and difficulty concentrating, especially at school, should also be alarms. Frequent physical complaints like stomachaches, headaches, and fatigue, as well as a sudden change in their grades, not completing homework, and losing interest in extracurricular activities may also be signs of depression that should be checked out. Another serious sign is reckless behavior, like driving fast or taking drugs and not caring if he or she lives or dies. One of the most serious signs of impending suicide is when a person has been depressed for a long time or has already had a suicide attempt and suddenly he or she cheers up. This could be a sign that he or she has made a decision to try to die.

WHAT YOU CAN DO IF SOMEONE IS SUICIDAL

When someone is thinking of suicide, try and encourage him or her to talk to a person who is trusted, such as a parent, a guardian, or a teacher.

Maybe he or she needs to talk to a guidance counselor, social worker, or someone in the mental health profession. If it would be more comforting, encourage your friend to talk to a spiritual adviser or a member of his or her clergy.

It is important to be a good friend and listen. Try to explore the problem: What has been going on in the past couple of months? What has led up to the current situation? Always take your friend seriously, and do not make jokes about his or her feelings. Be interested in his or her emotions and actions. Remember to remain calm and be non-judgmental, and offer appropriate options. If you think your friend is at risk, remove from his or her vicinity guns, pills, ropes, or anything else that could cause harm. Be there to offer any help or assistance. If it becomes over your head and the situation is turning into a crisis, tell a trusted adult. Remember, do not be sworn to secrecy. Seek help.

What you shouldn't do is debate whether suicide is right or wrong. Do not lecture on the value of life, and never dare the person to do it. Don't say:

- Don't worry, things will get better in time.
- It's not as bad as you think.
- You shouldn't feel that way.
- If you think you have it bad, listen to my problems!

Finally, do not leave a suicidal person alone. Call a responsible member of the family, a crisis help line, or if necessary, 911. You could save a life.

CHAPTER SEVEN

Coping with Depression and Suicide

THERE IS NO CLOSURE, NOR WOULD I WANT ONE. I WANT TO REMEMBER HIM ALL MY LIFE, VIVIDLY; HIS LAUGHTER, THE SMELL OF HIS SNEAKERS UNDER HIS BED, HIS MOMENTS OF JOY, HIS HUMILITY AND HIS INTEGRITY.

I f someone were to ask you right now, at this present moment, if you were having thoughts of suicide, what would your answer be? If the answer is "maybe" or "yes," then this is a really difficult time for you. There is no reason to go through this time alone. If talking to your parents is not possible, try confiding in a trusted friend or an adult who knows you. "I think that some of my teachers in high school are the reason I'm here today," says nineteen-year-old Helene.[1]

You may be starting to feel out of control and start experiencing sadness and signs of depression. You may feel that your life is a mess, lost and confused, that you have no effect on the outcome of your life, that your feelings are a blur, or you may be starting to have suicidal thoughts. When you are feeling suicidal, many times the emotional pain is great and you can feel isolated in your pain. A lack of adequate coping techniques can contribute to this sense of helplessness and hopelessness.

REACHING OUT FOR HELP

There are many teens who feel they would be rejected if people found out about their suicidal thoughts. Suicidal teens often hide their true feelings. Many times the teen feels that he or she has nowhere to go. The pain is unbearable, and the teen sees suicide as a choice. Here are some places where you can go for help before you take any further negative actions.

- Start at home with a parent or guardian, a friend's parent, or your clergy.
- If that is not working, see a guidance counselor, an empathetic teacher, or a coach. Talking to people you trust can also help support you. If you have a teacher whom you highly respect, tell him or her about your suicidal thoughts, even though it may be difficult. Take the risk. In most cases asking for help does get you the help you need.
- Make an appointment to see the school social worker, counselor, or psychologist as they are trained in suicide interventions.
- Certain hospitals have clinics for teens dealing with depression and suicide. You will need to look in the telephone book or on the Internet to see what clinics are in your hometown.
- Teen volunteers or peer counselors working at crisis centers ask questions of other teens using their own experiences and at a teenage level. By talking with them, it could possibly lead you to get counseling.
- Call a distress hotline. All conversations are confidential. These lines are manned by specially trained people to give you immediate support and can be helpful for you when you are in crisis. The people who man the hotlines are trained to listen to you. They have discussions with you and

learn about your problems and feelings of isolation. You can call back at any time if you feel suicidal or just need a helpful voice on the other end. They have had success in doing these immediate crisis interventions.

HANDLING STRESS

It is important for you to understand that you cannot eliminate stress entirely from your life, but you can learn how to manage it and reduce some of the distress it causes. You may not be able to control things, but you can control your reactions to those things. More positive ways to handle stress are through activities such as talking to someone who cares, exercising, listening to or playing music, and spending time with friends. When stressed, do you find yourself:

- Withdrawing into yourself?
- Resorting to self-abuse? (cutting, scratching until bleeding occurs, pulling out hair, bruising yourself, etc.)
- Resorting to self-destructive behaviors? (i.e., driving too fast)
- Using alcohol?
- Using drugs?
- Excessive risk taking?
- Directing anger to either a specific object or a person?

If you are handling stress in a number of these ways, you need to consider getting outside support to learn how to take better care of your emotional well-being. These supports could include a family member you trust, peer counseling, your family doctor, your spiritual adviser, social service agencies, your school guidance counselor, or professional therapy. If you are feeling depressed and suicidal, it is very important to talk to someone about what you are feeling. Finding someone to help is an act of wisdom and great courage. You may also feel relief that you have started to share your inner thoughts, feelings, and pain with someone who empathizes and will listen to your emotional struggles.

- Find someone comfortable talking about suicide and working with you to prevent the risk of these thoughts leading to suicidal actions.
- Don't give up. If the first person you approach does not provide the support you feel you need, find someone you feel will.
- Understand that the person you approach may need to refer you on to somewhere else. He or she may be honest with you and feel you need more support than what he or she can provide. He or she may see that you need someone who can prescribe medications to help you with your depression.
- The person will want to keep you safe. You may need to go to the hospital if you are at high risk to get the supports you need.

- Be honest with the person with whom you are dealing. Lies will just lead to more lies, and you will end up being caught up in them.

Getting Counseling

The most common method of dealing with suicidal behavior is doing some kind of talk therapy along with medication to help you through the depression. Counseling is a way to ask for help and talk about your problems with a trained therapist. It is objective, and the person cares what happens to you. It is a support to help you learn about yourself and how to cope. People go to counseling for many reasons, like family problems, problems at schools, feeling lonely, relationship difficulties, or just coping with the pressures of being a teenager.

Counselors are men and women who have been trained to listen to your concerns and problems and help you find some answers. Counselors can be psychologists, psychiatrists, social workers, guidance counselors, clergy people, and other trained individuals like nurses and doctors. Counseling is a process to learn about yourself, and it takes time and commitment. There are many types of counselors and treatments. You may need to shop around to get the person that best meshes with your personality.

Counseling tries to get you to help yourself go from one stage to another to lead a life without pain and sadness as the main focus. Private counseling usually takes place once or twice a week for one-hour sessions. You can discuss your emotions and try to come to some answers. If the therapist is a psychiatrist or a doctor who can prescribe medications, drug therapy may be offered, especially if he or she sees that you are feeling very depressed and very anxious. Doctors may recommend antidepressants to treat your depression. Antidepressant medication is used to correct a chemical imbalance or chemical disruption in a person's brain. A doctor has to write a prescription for the medication. There are many on the market, and the doctor may have you go through a series of trial medications before you find the one that is most appropriate for you. If you have an addiction to alcohol and/or drugs, a treatment facility may be offered as well.

A counselor may assess your risk of being suicidal. When you talk to a counselor, he or she will try to familiarize with your sources of stress and your coping mechanisms. A counselor will look for any suicidal warning signs that you may be exhibiting, and if he or she determines that you are at risk, he or she then can offer interventions to support you. All suicide signs are taken very seriously. If you have a suicide plan, be open and share it with your counselor. Also, your counselor needs to know if you have attempted suicide before. With his or her support, he or she will help you manage your stress and help monitor you so that you have somewhere to go if you are starting to feel that you are spiraling out of control.

Family counseling is meeting with the counselor and your family to talk about the individual and group dynamics in your family. This is a way to hear what each member in the family is saying and try to re-create family dynamics that will work for you in a more positive manner. Strengthening the family unit is the ultimate goal.

Group counseling is when you meet in a small group with others who have similar problems as you. It is a way to hear others who may share some of your own feelings. It also allows you an opportunity to offer your own perspective with peers your own age or people who have undergone similar traumas. Group therapy works well with many teens as it reaffirms their feelings that they are not the only ones who have these inner thoughts.

Getting a Therapist

To get a therapist, you usually need a referral. Your family doctor can give you one. There can be a cost for some therapists. This must be discussed with your family. Some therapists have sliding scales, and some are connected to agencies that may help you in your time of crisis.

Your parents might also have a drug or health plan that will cover the cost of your treatment. Again, sometimes you may need to shop around to get a therapist with whom you can connect.

Ten Great Questions to Ask a Therapist

1. What kind of therapy do you practice?
2. Are you also able to prescribe medications if I need them?
3. How much are your sessions?
4. What is the process of therapy, and what are the goals? How do you see me achieving them?
5. Do you think it is a good idea to keep a journal of my thoughts?
6. What happens if I feel uncomfortable in the sessions?
7. Are our sessions confidential? Will you tell my parents what I say?
8. Will you also be seeing other members of my family or peer group?
9. What will you do if I say I am feeling suicidal or I am having suicidal thoughts?
10. Do you have any good resources that you can recommend to me?

Peer Counseling

When regular high school students were given a choice of whom they would first confide in if they were having suicidal thoughts, 91 percent reported that they would confide in a friend before going to a parent, teacher, or other adult.[2] When interviewing high-risk students, the percentage went considerably lower as they reported that they would not confide in anyone. If adolescents are going to confide in anyone, their first choice appears to be a peer. Therefore, peer counseling may be the best type of situation for you to sort through your thoughts and troubles.

A number of schools have developed peer counseling programs. Much of what peer counselors are learning and teaching are interpersonal and social problem-solving skills, which are helpful to high-risk adolescents. During training, peer counselors are taught communication skills; alternatives for dealing with common problems such as family relations, breaking into student cliques, health problems, and peer relations; and the strategies and ethics of counseling. They may become a bridge between you and professionals. They are not there, however, to counsel you if you are contemplating suicide; they will refer you on to the appropriate professionals.

TREATMENT

When it comes to treatments for suicidal teens, the question that is always asked is what type of treatments and interventions are the most successful. There is really no straight answer, as each teenager is unique and reasons for treatment may vary.

It is possible that in some situations you need interventions and counseling, and with these techniques you will improve.

For some, a suicide attempt might be an out-of-character response to an acute stress in an otherwise normally adjusted young person. A thorough assessment and referral to the family doctor to monitor you may be all that is necessary. It is essential that a thorough assessment be done by a qualified specialist. You may need more than just monitoring. In dealing with many suicidal teens, one method of treatment might not be the answer. A combination therapy might be more useful.

Brief Crisis-Oriented Treatment

This treatment would be seen more at the school level. It involves five interrelated stages: assessment, problem solving, preventive measures, termination, and follow-up. In the first stage, the counselor would assess the risk of suicide. The second would be to see if you would be open to doing more of a problem-solving approach and including your parents or guardians. You would also have to agree to a no-suicide contract. Preventive measures could include further counseling from a specialist or if it was a school-related issue, maybe some psychological assessments. The counselor may use role playing to try and understand your way of dealing with your day-to-day problems. Your family may also be involved in the treatment so that everyone works together to help improve your emotional health. The counselor may then touch base at least once a week and extend the time frame if both feel you are on the road to recovery. Your family and you would have the counselor as your support person when and if needed once again. The crisis-oriented treatment works well only if you do not have problems like clinical depression or drug and alcohol abuse.

Psychodynamic Psychotherapy

Since suicide is not usually an impulse decision, many see that longer therapy is a better method for teenagers. Psychiatric treatment is usually a long-term process lasting longer than a year, suitable when the issues raised by clients are not ones that can be resolved instantly. Long-term psychiatric treatment enables a patient-therapist bond to develop. A trained therapist could then help you sort out your anger and conscious and unconscious behavior and help provide strategies for you to deal with them successfully. Unfortunately, schools cannot do long-term therapy, so you might need to be referred to a specialist in this field. There also may be a cost factor for long-term therapy depending on whether your family has health insurance.

Cognitive Behavioral Therapy

Many suicidal teens have these three negative views:

1. A negative view of themselves
2. A negative view of the world
3. A negative view of the future or a sense of hopelessness

The cognitive behavioral therapist would focus on your cognition, or how you see your own reality and interpret your world. The therapist would help you get insight into how you are seeing the world. The sessions usually last about twelve weeks, approximately twenty sessions or more. With this therapy, there also needs to be time to build rapport with the therapist.

Family Therapy

Some of the goals of family therapy are:

- Get you to see your place in the family
- Get you to see the family dynamics and make good changes
- Get your parents to understand the seriousness of the suicidal threat or attempt
- Get the whole family to work together in

an appropriate and supportive manner to help you
- Get your family to understand their conflicts and how to solve them among themselves.

Family therapy can be important in helping the teen but each member of the family must be willing to participate and work together to make the changes that need to be done. The family therapist is trained in understanding family dynamics.

Group Treatment

It does appear that a number of teens like to do group therapy with other teens. They have more in common with each other when it comes to the many stresses in their lives, like school and relationships. In order for group therapy to be successful, it has to be run by good leaders who can help support the dynamics between the individuals and the full group.

Psychopharmacological Therapy

When a doctor feels that you have a tendency toward depression, medication may be prescribed. Unfortunately, there is no "antisuicide" pill that can be prescribed to make the teen all better. There are antidepressant medications to stabilize your mood and relieve your symptoms, and there are other medications to control accompanying anxiety and excessive eating and sleeping. It appears that medication alone is not the sole answer in supporting the suicidal youth. You will probably need a combination of medication and talk therapy. Many drugs do have side effects, and so you'll need to be closely monitored. Since you could still be at a high risk for suicide, the access to the pills must be severely limited. School personnel would have to refer to a specialist who can assess and evaluate whether you need medication.

Other Supports Needed

Since you may have other problems, specialized treatment facilities or clinics may be needed. Treatments may include alcohol and drug abuse counseling and education. You may need to go to facilities (day treatment or residential) to get help with your abuse problems. If there is physical or sexual abuse at home, you can move into the home of a friend or other relative and get support from protection agencies in your town or city.

There are many different types of treatment. A person may need to do more than one to feel healthy again. The important thing to understand is that with treatment, a depressed person can get the help and supports needed to lead a productive life without emotional pain and to venture out of the dark abyss you may have been living in. With the treatments, you can have a chance at realizing that there are other ways to solve problems other than by taking your own life. There are well-trained people out there to help people cope with the day-to-day challenges of their lives.

AFTER A LOVED ONE COMMITS SUICIDE

Once a teen has committed suicide, many people are affected. The devastated family and friends are known as "survivors." There are millions of survivors each year trying to deal with the loss of their loved ones who died from suicide. Suicide survivors suffer in three ways: first, because they are grieving for the deceased; second, because they are suffering from the traumatic experience; and third, because people do not talk about suicide. Therefore, it is difficult to confide in your closest friends and family members and receive the response you may have received if it was another kind of death.

After a loved one has committed suicide you may go through a series of emotional ups and downs. You might experience initial shock. You might feel it is all a bad dream and when you wake up things will be back to normal. You might have bouts of crying, and feel blue and lethargic.

Your sleeping patterns may suffer as well. After a suicide, survivors within the family often experience feelings of guilt and often want to punish themselves for what has happened. You may torture yourself with thoughts about whether you could have done something different. If so, would the person be alive today? You may constantly ask or say to yourself:

- What if . . . ?
- Why didn't I . . . ?
- If only I could have . . .
- Suicide cheated me out of time to say good-bye.
- I had no chance to say "I'm sorry."
- I'm feeling helpless.
- I feel vulnerable. I'm afraid it will happen to others in my family.
- Why didn't I see the warning signs?
- Why? Why? Why?[3]

Many times in your head you will go over and over the last conversation or the last time you saw your loved one alive. You may start experiencing nightmares.

COPING WITH DEATH

One learns to live with the loss, the tragedy, the waste, and the gaping hole in the fabric of one's life. There is no closure, nor would I

*want one. I want to remember him all my life,
vividly; his laughter, the smell of his sneakers
under his bed, his moments of joy, his humility and his integrity.*[4]

Each person grieves differently and at his or her
own pace. Remember, you may not be at the same
stage as your other family members or friends.
There is no correct timing for grieving. Some people
may stay longer in certain stages than others.

- Denial (This isn't happening to me!)
- Anger (Why is this happening to me?)
- Bargaining (I promise I'll be a better
  person if . . .)
- Depression (I don't care anymore.)
- Acceptance (I'm ready for whatever comes.)

Communicating

It is important that you do not stay locked up in
your own emotions. Let them out. Cry. Talk to your
friends. You may need to take the initiative to talk
about the suicide or share your feelings. Many
people do not know what to say after a person
commits suicide. It may be important for you to
open the channels of communication. You may
find it helpful to reach out to family and friends.
Many times clergy is around the family to provide
comfort. This may be a time to look to your religion for some comfort.

Handling Your Feelings

Suicide is usually a culmination of a sequence of disturbing and troubling events. You may have been already living in a nightmare without control, and now that it is over there is a feeling of relief. You may feel ashamed for having these feelings.

There may also be a feeling of guilt, which might come from the relief that you feel that the person who committed suicide finally did it, guilty at not being able to stop the act, or guilty for blaming God. You may review the past and try and discover how you may have failed the person.

Many survivors also feel shame because the act of suicide is not condoned by their religion, town, family, or in general, society. You also may start blaming either yourself or others. You may experience symptoms of depression: disturbed sleep, loss of appetite, constant crying, waves of intense sadness, and general lack of energy. You may then need to seek help for yourself.

Dwelling on the suicide and picturing it in your head over and over is not beneficial. You may try to remember the kind and good acts of the deceased. The expectation that you will eventually find the "why" for the suicide is one of the first things you may have to give up on the way to healing. You cannot turn back the clock or erase the past. It is important to find someone or a group that you can relate to that will be a positive influence in your life and help you get to the stage of acceptance and support you through your grieving process.

Coping Within Your Family

If you have a sibling who committed suicide, you are a very vulnerable survivor. You must struggle with your own grief, as well as guilt, anger, sadness, and all other strong emotions. Unfortunately, your parents are also dealing with their own grief, and they may feel unfit as parents. They might want to give you the attention that you need but may not feel they have the strength to do it. You may start feeling neglected and troubled, or you might take on a parental role and view your parents as the children.

You need to be able to heal together as a family. Blaming each other will not help. Talking together and sharing emotions will be better for everyone in the long run.

If you have young siblings in your family, they may not understand the reactions around them. They may feel the death is their fault, or they may feel abandoned by their loved one. They, too, may benefit from children-oriented therapy, like play or art therapy.

Ways to Cope

If you have been affected by someone close to you who has committed suicide, bereavement groups are excellent for support. Information on finding one close to you can be found in the yellow pages of the phone book or on the Internet. Some are affiliated with local hospitals or medical centers. Many times members of these groups talk about their own experiences and learn how to live with their loss.

Eventually, you will laugh and enjoy your life again. You may have mixed emotions for feeling this way, but the process of healing will have started. The following are ways that may help you in your despair.

- Anniversaries, holidays, and birthdays may be difficult. You may feel intense sadness in the days leading up to these special events. You may want to create a ritual, like making a special card in honor of the loved one or visiting the grave and placing flowers on it. (Some people find going to the graveyard too depressing whereas others find it a refuge.)

- It is really important that you take care of your own personal well-being. You should eat right, exercise, and try to get enough sleep. This is not the time to take up risky behaviors like smoking, drinking, drugs, and sex just to drown out or not look at your feelings.

- You may need to go to a bereavement group or see a social worker, psychologist, psychiatrist, school guidance counselor, clergy person, or any professional person whom you feel comfortable enough to talk to and whom you feel can guide you through the therapeutic experience. There are also crisis intervention hotlines and centers that are staffed by trained personnel who offer guidance and support.

CHAPTER EIGHT

Prevention, Intervention, and Postvention

MANY PEOPLE SEEM TO FEEL THAT IF YOU DO NOT SEE IT OR HEAR ABOUT IT, IT WILL GO AWAY . . . BY COVERING UP SUICIDE AND PRETENDING IT IS NOT A MAJOR COMMUNITY CONCERN, ARE WE ACHIEVING SUCCESS?

Suicide is possibly the most preventable of all causes of death. The first step is to be able to talk and communicate feelings. To many families, the reaction to suicide is silence and pressure to keep it hidden. There are media blackouts or self-censorship when it comes to the publication of suicide stories. Many suicides, such as jumping off bridges or jumping in front of a subway train, are not reported for fear of copycat suicides. Many people seem to feel that if you do not see it or hear about it, it will go away. Family members do not discuss it openly. Children are not usually told the truth, and many would prefer to say the death was accidental rather than from suicide. By covering up suicide and pretending it is not a major community concern, are we achieving success? How can we prevent suicide from happening? Are there any ways?

Prevention can be seen as circular, involving three interconnected stages. Primary prevention aims to reduce the suicidal risk by concentrating on improving the physical, emotional, and spiritual well-being of at-risk people. Secondary prevention (early intervention) tries to target suicidal individuals either before they injure themselves or during a suicidal crisis. Tertiary prevention (postvention) focuses on individuals who have been affected by suicidal behavior: ones who have attempted it, those who are at high risk for recurrence, and family members who are also at high risk.

PREVENTION

Prevention is education. Research shows that educating parents, teachers, professionals, and the general public about the problem of suicide, what clues to look for, and where to get help is effective. Prevention programs include lessons on life skills and parenting, crisis hotlines, and support to high-risk families, and there are trained professionals to do screenings, assessments, and prevention work.

Suicide prevention education includes parental education. Teaching parents to learn about suicidal warning signs, the significance of developing their child's and their own self-esteem, developing trust with their child, and the need for parenting courses, especially on how to parent an adolescent, is part of the education. Peer education in schools could include topics like the warning signs of depression and suicide, how to deal with stress appropriately, sexuality, and what to keep confidential. Community education could also include warning signs like copycat suicides, developing community resources for teens, initiating suicide prevention programs, offering bereavement groups, and generally developing positive attitudes toward teens so they will seek help in their own communities. Teen self-education needs to include what leads up to suicide, how to cope, whom to talk to when they require help, and having access to school curriculum dealing with suicide.

There is compelling evidence indicating the treatment of alcohol and drug abuse can reduce suicide rates. Lessons about the hazards of substance abuse should also be addressed at school. Some effective interventions involve gun control. In a household in which a firearm is kept, it is almost five times more likely that an inhabitant will die from suicide than a person who is living in a gun-free home.[1]

USING THE INTERNET SAFELY

Even though chat rooms may seem like a good place to share your thoughts anonymously, you should be careful with whom you are chatting as that person may not have good advice for you.

If you are being bullied on the Internet, you need to save the evidence. Don't keep looking at it, as this may create more stress. You should store it in a place where you can access it later. Next, send an assertive message telling the bully to stop harassing you, and block or filter all messages from the bully.

If you've done those things, and the bully is still harassing you, change your e-mail address or IM user name, and tell your school counselor or teacher. If this doesn't stop the bully, you need to file a complaint either with the telephone company, if you're being harassed via cell phone, or with the Web site administrator (through the "contact us" link on the site). Ask the phone company or administrator to help you trace the identity of the bully.

Once you know who the cyberbully is, have your parent contact his or her parents or guardians to let them know what is going on. If you continue to be bullied, have your parent contact a lawyer to send a letter demanding the cyberbullying stop. Contact the police if the cyberbullying involves threats of violence, coercion, obscene messages, harassment or stalking, hate or bias messages, or if he or she is creating or sending sexually explicit pictures.

WHAT YOU CAN DO

Be aware of what you are posting on Web sites, including your own user name and personal home page. If you have a blog, be very careful what it contains. Go to an adult if you read anything online or have a circumstance that you feel uncomfortable handling yourself or if you are feeling threatened in any way.

In general, always guard your private contact information. Do not give people you do not know any information about yourself, like cell phone number, name, address, school, instant messaging name, or e-mail address. If you are being harassed online, stop the activity (leave the chat room, quit instant messaging), and tell an adult you trust. Block the sender's message—never reply to harassing messages—and save the harassing message. Show it to your parents, and send it to your Internet service provider, e.g., Hotmail, Yahoo!, etc.

If you have knowledge of others harassing somebody or you yourself are starting to become part of the group that is bullying somebody, stop it immediately. Tell an adult if you know somebody is harassing and hurting another person. Ask yourself if you would like it if somebody were treating you that way.

OVERCOMING SUICIDAL BEHAVIOR

The Teen Suicide Project at the University of Alberta, Canada, was created to investigate processes related to becoming suicidal and preventing suicide in adolescents. Its 2001 study looked at twelve- to nineteen-year-olds who were suicidal to find out what was helpful for them to overcome their thoughts of suicide, feelings, and behavior. The results indicated that if a person is feeling suicidal, it is important that he or she:

- Develop feelings of self-efficacy and personal worth through increased coping and problem-solving skills
- Increase social support, including having someone to listen to him or her
- Feel accepted despite his or her difficulties

To prevent teen suicide and for teens to overcome suicidal behavior, having personal connections and realizing that their struggles are normal appear to be critical components.

INTERVENTION

Intervention is the care and treatment of the person who is in crisis or who has suicidal concerns, and evaluating and managing a crisis situation. In school suicide intervention programs, the school develops systems to provide immediate help to high-risk students and establishes policies and procedures as well as links to outside community resources that do follow-up with students. Counseling in the school focuses on the severity of the student risk, and immediately prevents self-harm and stabilizes the student's current level of coping. There is a reduction in suicide rates of young people when there have been school-based interventions, such as crisis management, self-esteem enhancement, development of coping skills, and assistance in helping to make healthy decisions.

There are many ways to do interventions. Some of these treatments might start with a survey that determines a person's suicide risk level. A person may also start psychotherapy, which is a term used for different kinds of psychological counseling. Some methods include teaching people how to think positively and to develop coping and problem-solving skills. In therapy, a person may also undergo interpersonal therapy, which may include teaching social skills, such as making friends.

Psychotherapy doesn't have to be one on one. A person can join group therapy, meaning meeting people of the same age or with the same depressive illnesses. Family therapy is when everybody in your family participates in therapy sessions, either one on one or together as a family. There are also various supports at school, such as the school nurse, guidance counselors, psychologists, and social workers.

A person who is depressed can also use relaxation and visualization therapies, and biofeedback, which aims to correct stress level. Antidepressant medications and stimulants, perhaps alternative medications or vitamins such as Saint-John's-wort (all should be recommended and regulated by a medical practitioner), are other options to fighting depression.

HOSPITALIZATION

If the depression is severe enough, a person might require hospitalization. Once a suicide has been attempted, hospitalization may also be necessary. This may entail confinement in the psychiatric ward of a hospital and placing the patient on suicide watch and all staff on high alert. Although hospitalization may seem scary, it is a time in which specialists can help direct the next steps in preventing reoccurrence, like assessing for drug and alcohol abuse and understanding the risk factors. This is also a time that you may be treated with medications like antidepressants or antianxiety drugs as well as making sure you have somebody to go to for counseling when you leave the hospital. A 2005 study in WebMDHealth shows that a brief course of up to ten sessions of talk therapy compared with standard treatment (limited outpatient therapy, medication, and referral to an outside agency) reduced the risk of subsequent suicide attempts by up to 50 percent in people treated in hospital emergency rooms for attempted suicide.[2] The main goal of talk therapy is to identify the thoughts, images, and beliefs that are involved in prior suicidal attempts. The therapy involves addressing issues and helping the participants develop ways to adapt and cope with the stressors.

SUICIDE INTERVENTION PROGRAMS

Many schools have suicide awareness and intervention programs. The program may start by addressing what suicide is. You and your classmates may know or not know about suicide, including the myths, so some of the activities you might do include:

- Identifying whether statements are myths or facts

- Finding out whether each student knows somebody who has attempted suicide (rock stars or movie stars may be used)

You might also learn about how you can tell if someone is suicidal. This might be done by identifying what is normal adolescent emotional development, e.g. mood swings, from suicidal warning signs. Doing a role-playing exercise with a friend in which one person says how he or she is experiencing depression while the other friend reacts appropriately is also a good exercise.

There may be a discussion on why teens attempt suicide. Some of the discussion might focus on stress. For example, one activity is to pile a book on your opened hands after each person says something that is stressful to you. When you feel the weight is too much you say so. Another activity is to find a partner and both list all the stresses in your lives. Hook up with another group of two people and see if you match or can add more. At the end of the activity, you can list all the causes of stress and then talk about what you can all do to relieve stress.

These sessions might include a lesson on alcohol and drug abuse. A young adult who is recovering from abuse in the community could come to your school to talk about his or her experiences. It is important to talk about how you can help someone who is feeling suicidal. First, always try to be a good listener. Here are questions to ask yourself in evaluating your listening skills:

- Name a time when you were a good listener.
- Name a time when you were a poor listener.
- When did you pay attention?
- When were you too busy to pay attention?
- Did you make good eye contact?
- Were you distracted when somebody was trying to talk to you?
- Were you empathetic to somebody else's feelings?
- Were you interested in what somebody else had to say?

Suicide Prevention Activities

Make a video to show the contrasts of being an engaged listener and one who is disengaged in the conversation. Role-play guidance counselor and suicidal student; reverse roles.

It is important to emphasize how to get the most out of one's life. Some of the activities could include taking the time to look at yourself and see your strengths and needs. Look at what you enjoy and what makes the world worth living and what it is about your life that needs changing. You can work with a partner so that you can both brainstorm ways to make changes to see the world as a better place. Do an art activity or a hands-on activity that helps in celebrating who you are (a collage, a coat of arms, a spirit animal, a mask, etc.).

Doing research on people who have undergone undue hardships and could have committed suicide but chose not to and finding out why is also a good prevention activity. You could prepare a resource package that other teens can use when they need information and support. These packages could include portfolio items, stories, books, articles, beneficial Web sites, and a list of crisis centers and their numbers in the area.

POSTVENTION

The days and weeks after a suicide can be filled with confusion and turmoil. Postvention refers to the steps schools should take in the aftermath of a suicide to help the students, staff, and parents. After a student has committed suicide, coordinated services and activities designed to help students, parents, friends, teachers, and the community cope are necessary. The death of a student by suicide is very difficult for staff and students at the deceased's school. Some of the major concerns that need to be addressed are grief resolution and making sure that the imitative effect that a suicide death may have in a school community does not occur. Professionals can help support the family and friends who have been profoundly affected by the suicide of their loved one through individual and group counseling and support. High-risk students should be sought out to be counseled and monitored.

The funeral and memorial services should be handled with grace and dignity. It should be recognized that any student who commits suicide was part of the community and will be missed as his or her life had meaning and value.

Here's what you can expect when you work with a counselor after a suicide of a peer:

- Help you accept the reality of the loss. It is important to give yourself permission to grieve in your own way, as long as it is not detrimental to yourself or others.
- Help you to identify and express your feelings. You may have feelings of regret, anger, and guilt. Both positive and negative feelings may need to be expressed in a safe and empathetic environment.
- You may learn about typical grief reactions in an effort to normalize your experience. In the grieving process, there will be highs and lows, much like being on an emotional roller coaster.
- You may experience feelings of lack of control, which is not unusual.
- You may be cautioned against advice of not allowing yourselves to grieve or hurrying your grief process.

Remember that grief is individualistic, there is no right or wrong way to grieve. It may take you a long time to feel happy or even laugh again.

COMMUNITY RESPONSE TO SUICIDE

On March 11, 1987, four teenagers from a New Jersey community committed suicide by lock- ing themselves inside a 13-car garage and sitting in a car with the engine running . . . All four teenagers had trouble in school: three had dropped out of high school, and one had recently been suspended.[3]

Within days of the suicides, the community responded to prevent other suicides from occur- ring. School officials identified those they thought were at high risk, such as close friends of the deceased or those who had previously attempted suicide. They provided counselors for the students and a walk-in clinic manned twenty-four hours a day. Local police assisted in locating any person whom they thought was at high risk for attempt- ing suicide. The garage where the tragedy took place was locked and put under surveillance. The community made a plan to prevent cluster sui- cides. This "everyone is responsible" postvention response to the tragedy was praised.

WHAT YOU CAN DO TO MAKE A DIFFERENCE

If your school is not sensitized to or aware of the problem of suicide, here are some ideas to get started in the community.

- See if your school can start a peer counseling program.
- Make sure your school has guidelines in place for suicides, bullying, cyberbullying, high-risk behaviors, and depression.
- Find out what is already available in your community.
- Ask your local law enforcement agency about guidelines for restricting access to firearms for young people.
- Contact your local crisis line (most are in the telephone book), and ask what it has available in resources for education and training.
- Ask your local emergency services (paramedics, ambulances) about procedures and follow-up for people who attempt suicide.
- Create a Web site to inform individuals about service and resources.
- Help organize suicide awareness or intervention skills training.
- Get involved with staff at your school to create a suicide prevention plan.

CONCLUSION

The tragic fact about suicide is that it is permanent. There is no bringing back to life the person who has committed suicide. What can you do? Be aware of the warning signs. If you know a person who feels all alone, take a moment and find out why. If you see people who are depressed, take a moment to help get assistance for them. If you see people who are crying out for help, recognize their pain and help support them. Do not keep suicide under lock and key. Make a difference to another young life by offering your hand. If you are feeling suicidal yourself, seek help. Please take the hand that is being offered.

anorexia nervosa A serious eating disorder in which a person restricts his or her food intake.

assessment An evaluation, usually performed by a physician, of a person's mental, emotional, and social capabilities.

assimilation The process by which a minority group gradually adapts to the customs of the prevailing culture.

autocide A suicide disguised as an automobile accident.

bipolar Major mental disorder with episodes of mania and depression.

bisexual Having sexual attraction to both males and females.

chronic Lasting a long period of time.

clinical depression A state of depression so severe as to require treatment.

cluster suicides Two or more teen suicides that happen around the same time or in the same way; also called copycat suicides.

correlation A complementary relationship between things.

depression The condition of feeling sad and despondent.

disempowered Deprived of influence.

harass To irritate, torment.

heterosexual Being sexually attracted to people of the opposite sex.

hotline A call center in which professionals trained to help with a problem answer phone lines.

marginalization When somebody is cast in the low ranks of social standing.

mock To treat with ridicule.

neurological Dealing with the nervous system.

perinatal The period around childbirth.

pessimism A tendency to view the negative.

prenatal Existing or occurring before birth.

prevalent Commonly occurring.

psychiatry The branch of medicine that deals with the diagnosis, treatment, and prevention of mental and emotional disorders.

pyre A heap of combustibles for burning a corpse.

resolution A course of action to do something.

ritual A ceremonial act.

suicide The act of intentionally taking one's own life.

suicide rate The percentage of people in a specific group who take their own lives in a certain duration of time.

warning signs Specific observable behaviors, actions, and circumstances of an individual in crisis. These symptoms may indicate that the individual is at risk of suicide.

American Association of
  Suicidology (AAS)
4201 Connecticut Avenue NW
Suite 408
Washington, DC 20008
(202) 237-2280
Web site: http://www.
  suicidology.org

This national organization seeks to educate
and train suicide prevention professionals
to end the occurrence of suicide.

American Foundation for Suicide
  Prevention
120 Wall Street, 22nd Floor
New York, NY 10005
(888) 333-AFSP (2377)
Web site: http://www.afsp.org

This national nonprofit organization provides research and outreach for people who
may be at risk for suicide.

Centre for Suicide Prevention
1202 Centre Street SE, Suite 320
Calgary, AB T2G 5A5
Canada
Web site: http://www.suicideinfo.ca

This Canadian nonprofit organization
provides training and information on
suicide-related issues.

Suicide Awareness Voices of Education
9001 East Bloomington Fwy., Suite 150
Bloomington, MN 55420
(952) 946-7998
Web site: http://www.save.org

This nonprofit group mainly comprises survivors
of suicide.

World Health Organization
20 Avenue Appia
CH-1211 Geneva 27
Switzerland
Web site: http://www.who.int

This United Nations organization focuses on a range of global
health issues, including suicide.

Hotlines

Kids Help Phone: (800) 668-6868

National Fund for Depressive Illness:
(800) 245-4305

National Institute of Mental Health (NIMH):
(800) 421-4211

National Suicide Hotline: (800) SUICIDE (784-2433)

Youthline: (800) 246-4646

Videos

David's Story: A Teen Suicide, Sunburst Communications, 1991.

Seventeen-year-old David commits suicide. Now, in retrospect, those who knew him best try to figure out why they failed to see the violent act coming.

Friends for Life: Teen Suicide Prevention, Gerald T. Rogers Productions, 1987.

This film dramatically illustrates how several young people take the steps to confront friends who are depressed and might be candidates for suicide attempts.

WEB SITES

Due to the changing nature of Internet links, Rosen Publishing has developed an online list of Web sites related to the subject of this book. This site is updated regularly. Please use this link to access the list:

http://www.rosenlinks.com/ccw/suic

Ayer, Eleanor. *Teen Suicide: Is it Too Painful* (Issues of Our Time). Fairfield, IA: Twenty-First Century Books, 1997.

Berman, Alan L., David A. Jobes, and Morton M. Silverman. *Adolescent Suicide: Assessment and Intervention*. 2nd ed. Washington, DC: American Psychological Association, 2005.

Blauner, Susan Rose. *How I Stayed Alive When My Brain Was Trying to Kill Me*. New York, NY: HarperCollins, 2003.

Box, Matthew J. *Suicide*. San Diego, CA: Greenhaven Press, 2005.

Crook, Marion. *Teens Talk About Suicide*. Vancouver, Canada: Arsenal Pulp Press, 2004.

Elkind, David. *The Hurried Child: Growing Up Too Fast and Too Soon*. New York, NY: Basic Books, 2001.

Empfield, Maureen, and Nick Bakalar. *Understanding Teenage Depression: A Guide to Diagnosis, Treatment, and Management*. New York, NY: Henry Holt and Company, 2001.

Kübler-Ross, Elisabeth. *Working It Through: Workshop on Life,*

Death, and Transition. New York, NY: Scribner, 1997.

Levac, Anne Marie. *Helping Your Teenager Beat Depression: A Problem-Solving Approach for Families*. Bethesda, MD: Woodbine House, 2004.

Marr, Neil, and Tom Field. *Bullycide Death at Playtime*. Oxfordshire, England: Success Unlimited, 2000.

Murphy, James. *Coping with Teen Suicide*. New York, NY: Rosen Publishing, 1999.

O'Connor, Richard. *Undoing Depression: What Therapy Doesn't Teach You and Medication Can't Give You*. New York, NY: Penguin Group, 1999.

Peacock, Judith. *Teen Suicide*. Minneapolis, MN: Compass Point Books, 2005.

Roleff, Tamara L. *Teen Suicide*. San Diego, CA: Greenhaven Press, 2000.

Sperekas, Nicole B. *SuicideWise: Taking Steps Against Teen Suicide*. Berkeley Heights, NJ: Enslow Publishers, 2000.

Wallerstein, Claire. *Teen Suicide*. Chicago, IL: Heinemann Library, 2003.

Zeinert, Karen. *Suicide: Tragic Choice*. Berkeley Heights, NJ: Enslow Publishers, 1999.

American Academy of Pediatrics. "Some Things You Should Know About Preventing Teen Suicide." Retrieved July 6, 2006 (http://www.aap.org/advocacy/childhealthmonth/prevteensuicide.htm).

Anonymous. "Don't Let Gambling Cheat You Out of Your Youth." *LA Youth*. September–October 2002. Retrieved July 6, 2006 (http://www.layouth.com/modules.php?op = modload& name = Issue&action = IssueArticle&aid = 1618& nid = 14).

Arenofsky, Janice. "Teen Suicide." *Current Health 2*, Vol. 24, Issue 4, 1997.

Attwood, Tony. "Asperger's Syndrome." *Orphanet Encyclopedia*. February 2003. Retrieved July 6, 2006 (http://www.orpha.net/data/patho/GB/uk-asperger.pdf).

Berman, Alan, and David Jobes. *Adolescent Suicide Assessment and Intervention*. Washington, DC: American Psychological Association, 1991.

Board of Education for the City of Hamilton. *Suicide Prevention*. Hamilton, ON: The Salvation Army, 2002.

Burton, Nanette. *Understanding Depression and Suicide Student Workbook*. Santa Cruz, CA: Network Publications' Contemporary Health Series, 1990.

Canada Ministry of Health, Advisory Group on Suicide Prevention. *Acting on What We Know: Preventing Youth Suicide in First Nations*. 2001.

Centers for Disease Control and Prevention. "Suicide: Fact Sheet." March 30, 2006. Retrieved July 6, 2006 (http://www.cdc.gov/ncipc/factsheets/suifacts.htm).

Centre for Suicide Prevention. Retrieved June 27, 2006 (http://www.suicideinfo.ca).

Child Trends Databank. "Teen Homicide, Suicide, and Firearm Death." 2003. Retrieved July 6, 2006 (http://www.childtrendsdatabank.org/indicators/70ViolentDeath.cfm).

Crook, Marion. *Suicide: Teens Talk to Teens*. North Vancouver, Canada: Self-Counsel Press, 1997.

Cudnik, Doreen. "Why Did Robbie Kirkland Have to Die?" Healthyplace.com. Retrieved June 27, 2006 (http://www.healthyplace.com/communities/gender/gayisok/kirkland.html).

Davis, John M., and Jonathan Sandoval. *Suicidal Youth*. San Francisco, CA: Jossey-Bass Publishers, 1991.

Dolce, Laura. *The Encyclopedia of Health*. New York, NY: Chelsea House Publishers, 1992.

Donaleen, Saul. *Let's Live!* Vancouver, Canada: Council for the Family, 1992.

Flanders, Stephen A. *Suicide.* New York, NY: Facts on File, 1991.

Frymier, Jack. "Understanding and Preventing Teen Suicide: An Interview with Barry Garfinkle." *Phi Delta Kappan,* Vol. 70, No. 4, December 1988, pp. 290–293.

Hicks, Barbara Barrett. "Youth Suicide." Bloomington, IN: National Educational Service, 1990.

"Hispanic Teens More Likely to Attempt Suicide." MSNBC.com. June 8, 2006. Retrieved July 6, 2006 (http://www.msnbc.msn.com/id/ 13211254).

Huff, Cynthia O. "Source, Recency, and Degree of Stress in Adolescence and Suicide Ideation." *Adolescence.* Spring 1999. Retrieved July 6, 2006 (http://findarticles.com/p/articles/mi_m2248/ is_133_34/ai_54657531/pg_1).

Jackson, Helene. "Suicidal Behavior in Preadolescents." Retrieved July 6, 2006 (http:// www.columbia.edu/cu/csswp/journal/ news1997/suicidal.html).

Jacobson, Bertil, and Marc Bygdeman. "Obstetric Care and Proneness of Offspring to Suicide as Adults: Case-Control Study." *BMJ,* Issue 317, 1998, pp. 1346–1349.

Jamison, Kay Redfield. *Night Falls Fast: Understanding Suicide.* New York, NY: Vintage Books, 1999.

Johnson, S. W., and L. J. Maile. *Suicide and the Schools*. Springfield, IL: Charles C. Thomas Publisher, 1987.

Johnson, Wanda Y. *Youth Suicide*. Bloomington, IN: Phi Delta Kappa Educational Foundation, 1999.

Kirk, William, G. *Adolescent Suicide*. Champaign, IL: Research Press, 1993.

Kuklin, Susan. *After a Suicide: Young People Speak Up*. New York, NY: G. P. Putnam's Sons, 1994.

Lukas, Christopher, and Henry M. Seiden. *Silent Grief: Living in the Wake of Suicide*. New York, NY: Scribner's, 1987.

McElvaine, Robert S. *The Great Depression: America, 1929–1941*. New York, NY: Times Books, 1993,

Media Awareness Network. Retrieved July 7, 2006 (http://www.media-awareness.ca/english/index.cfm).

Ministry of Health, the New Zealand Youth Suicide Prevention Strategy. "Suicide and the Media, the Reporting and Portrayal of Suicide in the Media, a Resource." Wellington, New Zealand, 1999.

National Center for Injury Prevention and Control. "Suicide Fact Sheet." Retrieved July 7, 2006 (http://www.cdc.gov/ncipc/factsheet/suifacts.htm).

National Institute of Mental Health. "Depression." July 3, 2006. Retrieved July 6, 2006 (http://www.nimh.nih.gov/healthinformation/depressionmenu.cfm).

National Mental Health Association. "Mental
Health: Pay for Services or Pay a Greater Price."
Retrieved July 6, 2006 (http://www.nmha.org/
shcr/community_based/costoffset.pdf).

O'Connor, Richard. *Undoing Depression: What
Therapy Doesn't Teach You and Medication Can't
Give You.* New York, NY: Penguin Group, 1999.

Pfeiffer, Cynthia. *The Suicidal Child.* New York, NY:
Guilford Press, 1986.

Pollack, W. *Real Boys: Rescuing Our Sons from
the Myths of Boyhood.* New York, NY: Henry
Holt, 1998.

Portner, Jessica. "Complex Set of Ills Spurs Rising
Teen Suicide Rate." *Education Week*, Vol. 19,
Issue 31, 2000.

Portner, Jessica. *One in Thirteen: The Silent Epidemic
of Teen Suicide.* Beltsville, MD: Gryphon House
Inc., 2001.

Portway, Suzannah, and Barbara Johnson. "Do
You Know I Have Asperger's Syndrome?"
Health Risk and Society, Vol. 7, No. 1,
March 2005.

Religious Tolerance.org. "Suicide Among Canada's
Native People." March 2, 2001. Retrieved July 6,
2006 (http://www.religioustolerance.org/
sui_nati.htm).

Salk, Lee, P. Lipsett, Sturner Lewis, Q. William,
Bernice M. Reilly, and Robin H. Levat.
"Relationship of Maternal and Prenatal
Conditions to Eventual Adolescent Suicide."
Lancet, Vol. I, March 16, 1985, pp. 624–627.

Schemo, Diana Jean. "Indians in Brazil Wither in an Epidemic of Suicide." *New York Times.* August 25, 1996. Retrieved June 27, 2006 (http://query. nytimes.com/gst/fullpage.html?sec = health& res = 9C05E1D81439F936A1575BC0A960958260).

Schleifer, Jay. *Everything You Need to Know About Teen Suicide.* New York, NY: Rosen Publishing,1997.

Smith, Judie. *Coping with Suicide.* New York, NY: Rosen Publishing, 1986.

Smolin, Ann, and John Guinan. *Healing After the Suicide of a Loved One.* New York, NY: Simon & Schuster, 1993.

Stephens, B. J. "Suicidal Women and Their Relationships with Their Parents." *Omega,* Vol. 16, No. 4, 1986, pp. 289–299.

Tantam, Mark. "Computers in Court—The Story So Far." *Law Society Gazette,* 1988.

Warner, Jennifer. "Therapy Can Prevent Repeat Suicide Attempts." WebMD.com. August 2, 2005. Retrieved July 6, 2006 (http://www.webmd.com/ content/article/109/109323.htm).

Wasserman, Ira. "Imitation and Suicide: A Reexamination of the Werther Effect." *American Sociological Review,* Issue 49, June 1984, p. 428.

Willard, Nancy E. "Cyberbullying and Cyberthreats: Responding to the Challenge of Online Social Cruelty, Threats, and Distress." February 24, 2006. Retrieved July 6, 2006 (http://www.doe. state.in.us/isssa/cyber_ bullying.html).

Wissow, Lawrence S., et al. "Cluster and Regional Influences on Suicide in a Southwestern American Indian Tribe." *Social Science and Medicine*, Vol. 53, 2001, pp. 1115–1124.

World Health Organization. "Suicide Huge but Preventable Public Health Problem, Says WHO." September 8, 2004. Retrieved July 6, 2006 (http://www.who.int/mediacentre/news/releases/2004/pr61/en).

Chapter 1

1. Encyclopaedia Britannica. "Masada," September 1, 2006. Retrieved August 31, 2006 (http://search.eb.com/eb/article-9051235?query = masada&ct = eb).
2. Diana Jean Schemo, "Indians in Brazil Wither in an Epidemic of Suicide." *New York Times*, August 25, 1996.
3. Robert S. McElvaine, *The Great Depression: America, 1929–1941*. Retrieved July 17, 2006 (http://www.nps.gov/elro/glossary/great-depression.htm).
4. World Health Organization. "Suicide Huge but Preventable Public Health Problem, Says WHO." September 8, 2004. Retrieved July 6, 2006 (http://www.who.int/mediacentre/news/releases/2004/pr61/en).
5. National Center for Injury Prevention and Control. "Suicide: Fact Sheet." March 30, 2006. Retrieved July 6, 2006 (http://www.cdc.gov/ncipc/factsheets/ suifacts.htm).

Chapter 2

1. Cynthia O. Huff, "Source, Recency, and Degree of Stress in Adolescence and Suicide Ideation," *Adolescence*, Spring 1999. Retrieved July 6, 2006 (http://findarticles.com/p/articles/mi_m2248/is_133_34/ai_54657531/pg_1).
2. National Mental Health Association, "Mental Health: Pay for Services or Pay a Greater Price." Retrieved July 6, 2006 (http://www.nmha.org/shcr/community_based/costoffset.pdf).
3. Public Health Service, "Depression and Suicide in Children and Adolescents," *Mental Health: A Report of the Surgeon General.* Retrieved August 29, 2006 (http://www.surgeongeneral.gov/library/mentalhealth/chapter3/sec5.html).
4. Brenda High. jaredstory.com. Retrieved August 18, 2006 (http://jaredstory.com).

Chapter 3

1. Ann Quigley, "Sex and Drug Use Increase Teen Suicide Risk." Health Behavior News Service, September 10, 2004. Retrieved August 28, 2006 (http://www.cfah.org/hbns/news/teensuicide09-10-04.cfm).
2. Anonymous, "Don't Let Gambling Cheat You Out of Your Youth," *LA Youth*, September–October 2002. Retrieved July 6, 2006 (http://www.layouth.com/modules.php?op=modload&name=Issue&action=IssueArticle&aid=1618&nid=14).

3. B. J. Stephens, "Suicidal Women and Their Relationships with Their Parents," *Omega*, Vol. 16, No. 4, 1986, pp. 289–299.
4. American Academy of Pediatrics, "Some Things You Should Know About Preventing Teen Suicide." Retrieved July 6, 2006 (http://www.aap.org/advocacy/childhealthmonth/prevteensuicide.htm).
5. Helene Jackson and Annaclare van Dalen, "Suicidal Behavior in Preadolescents." Retrieved July 6, 2006 (http://www.columbia.edu/cu/csswp/journal/news1997/suicidal.html).
6. Lee Salk, Lewis P. Lipsett, William Q. Sturner, Bernice M. Reilly, and Robin H. Levat, "Relationship of Maternal and Prenatal Conditions to Eventual Adolescent Suicide," *Lancet*, Vol. 1, March 16, 1985, pp. 624–627.
7. Bertil Jacobson, and Marc Bygdeman, "Obstetric Care and Proneness of Offspring to Suicide as Adults: Case-Control Study," *BMJ*, Vol. 317, 1998, pp. 1346–1349.

Chapter 4

1. Nancy E. Willard, "Cyberbullying and Cyber-threats: Responding to the Challenge of Online Social Cruelty, Threats, and Distress," February 24, 2006. Retrieved July 6, 2006 (http:// www.doe.state.in.us/isssa/cyber_bullying.html).
2. Centre for Suicide Prevention. Retrieved June 27, 2006 (http://www.suicideinfo.ca).

3. Simon Castles. "A Sad History of LIfe—and Death—Imitating Art." *The Age*, August 20, 2006. Retrieved August 28, 2006 (http://www.theage.com.au/news/opinion/a-sad-history-of-life-8212-and-death-8212-imitating-art/2006/08/19/1155408067969.html).

4. Ira M. Wasserman, "Imitation and Suicide: a Reexamination of the Werther Effect," *American Sociological Review*, No. 49, June 1984, p. 428.

5. W. Pollack, *Real Boys: Rescuing Our Sons from the Myths of Boyhood* (New York, NY: Henry Holt, 1998).

6. Jessica Portner. *One in Thirteen: The Silent Epidemic of Teen Suicide* (Beltsville, MD: Gryphon House, 2001).

Chapter 5

1. Associated Press, "Hispanic Teens More Likely to Attempt Suicide," MSNBC.com, June 8, 2006. Retrieved July 6, 2006 (http://www.msnbc.msn.com/id/13211254).

2. Louis Brown, "The Home Front Stopping: Suicide," *Toronto Star*, March 25, 2006.

3. National Center for Injury Prevention and Control. "Homicide and Suicide Among Native Americans, 1979–1992." Retrieved June 27, 2006 (http://www.cdc.gov/ncipc/pub-res/natam.htm).

4. Religious Tolerance.org, "Suicide Among Canada's Native People," March 2, 2001.

Retrieved July 6, 2006 (http://www.
religioustolerance.org/sui_nati.htm).

5. Marie Wadden, "Addiction, Suicide Return,"
Toronto Star, December 13, 2005.

6. L. S. Wissow, et al., "Cluster and Regional
Influences on Suicide in a Southwestern
American Indian Tribe," *Social Science and
Medicine*, Vol. 53, 2001, pp. 1115–1124.

7. Healthy Place.com, "Suicide Among Blacks."
Retrieved July 6, 2006 (http://www.
healthyplace.com/communities/depression/
minorities_5.asp).

8. Dwan "Telly" Carter. "The Truth About Black
Teen Suicide," November 10, 2000. Retrieved
July 17, 2006 (www.youthcomm.org/NYC%
20Features/Black%20Suicide(11-10-00).htm).

9. Doreen Cudnik, "Why Did Robbie Kirkland
Have to Die?" *Gay People's Chronicle*, February 21,
1997. Retrieved June 27, 2006 (http://www.
healthyplace.com/communities/gender/
gayisok/kirkland.html).

10. Public Health—Seattle and King County, "Gay,
Lesbian, Bisexual and Transgender Health,"
December 5, 2003. Retrieved July 6, 2006
(http://www.metrokc.gov/health/glbt/
youthsafety.htm).

Chapter 7

1. Janice Arenofsky, "Teen Suicide," *Current
Health 2*, Vol. 24, Issue 4, 1997.

2. The Board of Education for the City of Hamilton, *Suicide Prevention* (Hamilton, ON: The Salvation Army, 2002), p. 82.
3. Christopher Lukas and Henry M. Seiden, *Silent Grief: Living in the Wake of Suicide* (New York, NY: Scribner's, 1987).
4. American Foundation for Suicide Prevention, "Coping with Suicide Loss." Retrieved August 21, 2006 (http://www.afsp.org/index.cfm?page_id = FED822A2-D88D-4DBD-6E1B55D56C229A75).

Chapter 8

1. National Center for Health Statistics at the Centers for Disease Control and Prevention. "Refuse to Suffer." Retrieved August 28, 2006 (http://www.lollie.com/blue/suicide4.html).
2. Jennifer Warner, "Therapy Can Prevent Repeat Suicide Attempts," WebMd.com, August 2, 2005. Retrieved July 6, 2006 (http://www.webmd.com/content/article/109/109323.htm).
3. CDC, "Epidemiologic Notes and Reports Cluster of Suicides and Suicide Attempts—New Jersey," MMWR Weekly. Retrieved September 18, 2006 (http://iier.isciii.es/mmwr/preview/mmwrhtml/00000009.htm).

ABOUT THE AUTHOR

Sandra Giddens has been both a special education consultant and coordinator in the Toronto District School Board dealing with students with special needs, including teens with Asperger's syndrome, with learning disabilities, and suffering from depression. She cochairs the parent association of her son's high school and brings in guest speakers to talk about teen issues, some of which can lead to suicide, such as anorexia, depression, anxiety, and bullying on the Internet, as well as parenting a teenager. She presently is part of a multidisciplinary team dealing with autism. She has written a number of books for Rosen Publishing, including *Coping with Grieving and Loss*.

Photo Credits: Cover, p. 1 © www.istockphoto.com

Designer: Nelson Sá; Editor: Jun Lim